MW01248048

A Better I

When a Woman Loves God

Eartha L. Mims

Xulon Press

Xulon Press
2301 Lucien Way #415
Maitland, FL 32751
407.339.4217
www.xulonpress.com

© 2023 by Eartha L. Mims

All rights reserved solely by the author. The author guarantees all contents are original and do not infringe upon the legal rights of any other person or work. No part of this book may be reproduced in any form without the permission of the author.

Due to the changing nature of the Internet, if there are any web addresses, links, or URLs included in this manuscript, these may have been altered and may no longer be accessible. The views and opinions shared in this book belong solely to the author and do not necessarily reflect those of the publisher. The publisher therefore disclaims responsibility for the views or opinions expressed within the work.

Unless otherwise indicated, Scripture quotations taken from the King James Version (KJV) – *public domain*.

Paperback ISBN-13: 978-1-66287-979-1
Ebook ISBN-13: 978-1-66287-980-7

Dedication

In memory of my parents John Wesley and Willie Mae Brown for the Christian examples set before and always believing in me to have a positive influence on others.

Preface

Throughout the centuries, women have endured many challenges along their journey from equal rights to valuing themselves. The successes and failures these women experience along their journeys can influence individuals and society for eternity, beginning as far back as the garden of Eden and leading all the way to the present-day. Women underestimate or exploit this precious gift of influence they have to upbuild or dismantle a nation; however, when a woman loves God, every decision made regarding singleness, marriage, career, and so forth is influenced by her love for God. The world's views may influence her for a brief moment, but the influence of God in her life will prevail.

When a woman accepts Jesus Christ has her personal Savior, the lens she looks through is transformed from the world to God's view. She prays for God's direction regarding all life decisions and obeys His commands. The Holy Spirit compels her to do it God's way, and when she does, no regrets will follow on her Christian journey. The influence of this world may overpower her for a brief moment, but the power of the Holy Spirit will direct her back to her love for God. The influence of the Holy Spirit guides her from the moment of acceptance, young or old, to live for God. Accepting Jesus

Christ at a young age and applying His teachings will prevent many hardships of life such as promiscuity or the use of drugs or alcohol.

When a woman sins against God or fails to heed to the Holy Spirit, God will forgive, but be mindful. God knows our hearts and every motive that is concealed from the world. When we ask for forgiveness, God knows when it is genuine, which is true repentance. True repentance is feeling sorrowful for a negative behavior committed and asking God for strength and courage to turn away from it.

Be blessed and inspired as you read!

Table of Contents

Introduction

Have you ever had a deep, longing feeling of knowing there is something you needed to do? This feeling, or prompt, can linger for years, yet you do not have a clue what it is. You continue to do what you think you need to do in the interim, but in the back of your mind, you know there is something else.

Many years have passed since I received my first prompting. At that time, my children were very young, and I asked to allow my children to be self-sufficient before I started my journey. After my request to the Lord, I would sometimes feel the prompting very strongly, especially after hearing or seeing an individual's story about doing something to help others to improve or overcome an adversity.

When my youngest was about two years old, I when back to college to get a master's degree in educational leadership in 2001. I wanted to become a principal of an elementary or middle school. I completed my course work December 2005, taking one course at a time. I took the educational leadership state test and surprised myself by passing it on my first try. There were many internal roadblocks I faced during that time, but I thank God that I did not become bitter and allowed His truth to set me free.

But I say unto you, Love your enemies, bless them that curse you, do good to them that hate you, and pray for them which despitefully use you, and persecute you; Matthew 5:44

At that point, I decided to wait until my youngest child completed middle school before seeking employment at another school in the district to gain the support to become an assistant principal. During my youngest's last year in middle school in 2011, I felt an extraordinary prompt to further my education. There were times I felt like I was fighting with God and gave Him every logical excuse I could find. My oldest child was in his last year of high school with my second child two years behind him and both were going to college. Yet self-doubt arose in my mind as I began to think someone else out there was better equipped than myself to return to school. Not to mention my age and close to retirement caused even further doubt in myself. I was restless day and night for three months.

After visiting my family in South Carolina and returning to Florida, I visited a local university to gain information about their doctorate program. It was that visit when I finally received peace. I completed and submitted the paperwork by the deadline for acceptance into the August 2012 semester; however, in March 2012, I received a letter from the university stating I was a good candidate, but that there were "better applicants." To be honest, I was actually excited to receive the letter of non-acceptance and stated in my mind, *It was not from God.*

A month or two passed. Then one day on my way to work, a testimony my brother had given addressed my situation. My brother, a pastor of a small congregation, wanted to build an educational building. The church consulted financial agencies for the money to build, but received an answer of "no" due to the church's small congregation. My brother persisted and told the church he felt led to pursue the endeavor. After many more "nos" from many other financial institutions, he found himself having a casual conversation with one of the church's business associates and was offered the money after all of the paperwork was completed.

I had a casual conversation of my own with a friend in July 2012. She talked about one of her co-workers working on her doctorate, and the bells went off in my head. I did not say anything to my friend, but looked up the institution she had mentioned after arriving home. The university was holding an informational session that Saturday! I went and the director there asked me when I was thinking about starting. I told her August 2013, but then she asked, "How about now? This August 2012 semester?" I was shocked and couldn't believe what she said. She continued by saying, "If you meet all of the requirements, I will work with you to get you in for this fall."

While I was excited after leaving the university, I thought, *No way will my husband agree to borrow the money I need to attend.* Deep down, I really wanted him to say "no." I knew God would not want me to bring this financial obligation without my husband agreeing. After arriving home, I told my husband about the session and the financial assessment. My husband surprised me with his answer. "If you feel you have been called to do this, I will not be the one to stand in your way." My last hope of turning around and not working on my doctorate was my thought of my husband's response of "no" that ended up being a "yes" instead.

I finally surrendered to do the work God was calling me to do. I completed all of the paperwork, turned it in, and was accepted into their program for August 2012. The process was demanding, but God was with me through every aspect of the program. He placed people in my life to encourage and guide me through the doctoral process. I completed the program in Spring 2017. Several weeks later, I felt God's Spirit telling me I was going to write. Writing was one of my challenging areas of academics, so I believed I would write an article for a magazine or newspaper or something, but even after I received the prompting about writing, I still felt lost.

Upon completing my doctorate, I still wanted to pursue an assistant principal position, but felt my interest deteriorating. I decided to contact my county's school district in August 2017 regarding what I needed to do to be considered and placed into the assistant principal pool for interviews. After sending the new director of professional development copies of my prior final information, he indicated I did not have to take the county courses over, but needed to do the last requirement, which I had already completed. He then gave me an individual to contact in his office to schedule a time to complete the process. The individual encouraged me to take one course as a refresher, so I did. The course ran from September 2017 to November 2017.

After completing the course, I realized the additional training I had requested and had been given by my supervisor during that semester was just busy work; it did not have value for the final requirement for an assistant principal opportunity. Nevertheless, I was going to sign-up for the final process. All applicants who completed the course were given a window to contact the director's secretary to sign up for the final stage, yet I was directed by the Holy Spirit *not* to sign-up. Again, I was planning to try and request activities to prepare myself for the final stage. I also knew my yearly income would decrease due to the county's formula for new assistant principals. I spoke with long-time school principal who advised me to keep doing what I was doing and find an adjunct position at a college or university. I was still unsure what to do. As time when by, I lost complete interest in pursuing an assistant principal job.

I spoke with my pastor after a Bible study class about knowing your calling. He stated, "God is not the problem", so I did some soul searching. I asked God to help me to know my calling and He answered me by, once again, telling me to write, a book this time. I knew it would be about women and their relationship with God. In the summer of 2018, I started writing this book, focusing on singleness and marriage. After completing the outline on singleness and marriage, God's Spirit surprised me with the other chapter topics, a direction I would not have taken. He also introduced special individuals into my life to inspire me with other chapters.

May the following pages offer spiritual comfort, support, and guidance for whatever stage of life you find yourself.

Chapter 1

Singleness

A **single woman** who loves God has many struggles to overcome, especially if she wants a family. As the years pass and Mr. Right is nowhere to be found, many women start accepting men who do not have a relationship with God and have no desire to know Him. The Bible speaks of being unequally yoked in 2 Corinthians 6:14. *Be ye not unequally yoked together with unbelievers: for what fellowship hath righteofus with unrighteousness? and what communion hath light with darkness?* Michelle Hammond's book *What to Do Until Love Finds You*[1] infers developing a deep relationship with Jesus will enable you to discern a man's character and listen to what the Holy Spirit is revealing about the individual. Through the Holy Spirit, you will spend less time in meaningless relationships and heartbreaking experiences.

In the Book of Genesis, God promised Abraham and Sarah a son to carry on the family's name; however, Sarah became anxious due to her age and decided to allow her handmaid to bear her husband a child. When we walk out of the will of God, we suffer many consequences now and forever. Sarah despised her handmaid after she gave birth to the child and told her husband to send them from their camp. Sarah's decision had an everlasting impact on her and generations afterwards.

Single women must wait on the Lord and be of good courage. I believe Psalm 27:14 states it best. *Wait on the Lord: be of good courage, and he shall strengthen thine heart: wait, I say, on the Lord.* A blog posted by The Praying Woman Blog indicated "7 Dating Principles Single Christian Women Should Apply Daily"[2]:

1. "Put on the armor of God daily"–Pray and apply God's Word daily
2. "Allow the Holy Spirit to direct and lead you"–Pray and request God to guide you in all aspects of your life
3. "Put obedience over passion"–Allowing God's truth to prevail over physical desires
4. "Examine your personal motives"–Pressure from friends, family, or the world/ loneliness or self-image
5. "Be guided by love versus lust"–Love generates self-control not self-fulfillment
6. "Define your values"–Clear understanding of what is important and possible responses for difficult situations
7. "Do not be unequally yoked"–What commonality does righteousness have with lawlessness or darkness with light?

A single woman must preserve her body from many negative sensual influences such as touch, visual stimulations, and music. These devices can be utilized in a negative manner, especially to a single woman trying to live her life according to God's Word. Intense touching between an unmarried couple is the playground of many regrets. Decisions are made due to the passion that lies between the two individuals. This passion is a precious gift from God which is designed for marriage, so women and men should avoid putting themselves into a position to fall prey to sin by setting touching boundaries before starting a relationship with the opposite gender. If the individual does not respect another's touching boundaries, maybe the relationship was not meant to be at that time.

Single women should avoid all visual stimulations with a sexual condensation such as pictures, movies, and television shows. These imageries may trigger unwanted desires that can lead to ungodly living. There are many rules human beings create to justify ungodly behavior such as the three-, ten-, and thirty-day "date rules" before becoming sexually involved. God states this regarding sexual relationships as it is intended for married individuals (1 Corinthians 7:2). Anything outside of the marriage bedroom is sin and grieves God. Single women are called to live a life that is pleasing to God by keeping their body holy and abstaining from sex until marriage. It will be a difficult journey for single sexually active women, but God can sustain them with determination and a willing heart.

> Know ye not that your bodies are the members
> of Christ? shall I then take the members of Christ,
> and make them the members of an harlot? God
> forbid. What? know ye not that he which is joined
> to an harlot is one body? for two, saith he, shall

be one flesh. But he that is joined unto the Lord is one spirit. Flee fornication. Every sin that a man doeth is without the body; but he that commit- teth fornication sinneth against his own body. 1 Corinthians 6:15-18

Listening and dancing to seductive music has the ability to awaken the dormant libido. It is a precious gift from God that is beautiful and honorable if utilized within the confines of marriage. Unmarried women should avoid the sensation of this powerful force by not having any physical contact or engaging in dances that promote sexual temptation. The energy the music creates could set up Christian women for a great fall and many regrets, so it is probably best not to test one's will power.

A book written by Joy Jacobs and Deborah Strubel titled *Single, Whole and Holy: Christian Women and Sexuality*[3] posed four explanations regarding "Planning to Fail or Failing to Plan?" to assist in remaining holy as a single woman:

1. "Can you express why you wish to remain a virgin or renew sexual abstinence? Put your thoughts in writing in the form of a purpose statement."
2. "Base your purpose statement on Scripture (suggested verses: 1 Corinthians 6:13-17, 10:8; Ephesians 5:3; 1 Thessalonians 4:3-8)."
3. "What specifically do you need to do in order to starve Satan out of any strongholds he might have in your life?"
4. "The Bible says that your life is like a letter from God to the world. What does your letter say?"

Finally, many churches offer singles ministries to give support to unmarried believers. Some single groups may exhibit character traits that may hinder one's growth to live a life of celibacy. Some people have only one objective, to find a mate and not a better understanding of the things in the Lord. An article written by Alex Florea for Boundless.org,[4] "6 Characteristics of a Healthy Singles Ministry," focused on the family ministry by indicating six qualities to look for in a singles ministry:

1. "It is devoted to studying God's Word"
2. "It is accountable to a local church"
3. "It discourages consumerism"
4. "It facilitates fellowship"
5. "It is shepherded by a plurality of diverse leaders"
6. "It produces godly marriages"

These are all good attributes of a stable, God-fearing, and personal growth ministry, though Florea indicated he could not guarantee number six.

If you are planning on attending a singles ministry, ask questions about the ministry's initiatives to seek answers from the group's leader/s. After attending and you observe questionable attributes that do not uphold kingdom principles, search for another group, and ask God what direction He would have you go. If you do not receive an answer immediately, continue or start to participate in a Bible study and Sunday school at your church or a local church. This may be all you need to maintain the life God has called you to at this moment in your life.

The lust of the flesh has caused many women to experience unnecessary pain and frustration.

This I say then, Walk in the Spirit, and ye shall not fulfil the lust of the flesh. Galatians 5:16

Now the works of the flesh are manifest, which are these; Adultery, fornication, uncleanness, lasciviousness... Galatians 5:19

If you are or have been sexually active as a single woman, you are going to have a challenging time distancing yourself from a sexual relationship, but know that all things are possible with God if your desires are pure. You may fall, but learn to distance yourself from the situation that may cause you not to succeed. It may take a year for the lust to subside or maybe only a few months. Just always remember Joseph in Genesis 39:12, *And she caught him by his garment, saying, Lie with me: and he left his garment in her hand, and fled, and got him out.* If you find yourself in a situation that may cause you to stumble, flee like Joseph. Also remember that God gives us a way of escape (1 Corinthians 10:13), and Hebrews 2:18, *For in that he himself hath suffered being tempted, he is able to succour them that are tempted.*

It is time to live the way that is pleasing to God and receive His many blessings. Again, your situation may be or will be challenging, but the Holy Spirit is there to guide and keep you. The Word states that lust will pass away, but doing the will of God will last forever (1 John 2:16-17).

Chapter 2

Marriage

Married women should conduct themselves honorably at all times. She should bring honor to her husband, household, conduct, and interaction with others. She is admired for how she shows love toward her family and those in need. She is not self-centered, but open to hear the directions of her Heavenly Father. She will not do anything to hurt or harm her husband, and looks for his best welfare in all things. In return, her husband loves and respects her. Her husband and children compare her to the virtuous woman in Proverbs 31. A married woman who loves God in words and deeds strives for these virtues in a marriage.

Before entering into marriage, a single woman should seek God's approval of the union. Physical attraction plays an important role, but is not the absolute reason to say "yes" to a knight in shining armor. Over time, the young man's physique will evolve and you need to know him for his spirituality and his love for God, as he will learn about you. Do not claim something you do not know, but consult God as you date and refrain from sexual intimacy until marriage.

After marrying your knight, do not refrain from sexual intimacy unless agreed upon. A woman who loves God brings honor and respect to the marriage and their children's children are blessed.

When a married woman enters into marriage, she wants to please God first, then her husband. If she loves God and has the desire to please Him, she will please her husband. What do I mean by pleasing her husband?

First, she will love him unconditionally and give herself to him freely without conditions. Remember, the two shall become one flesh (Mark 10:8); your body is his and his body is yours. Leave no room for adversary to creep and destroy the beautiful union. There will be nights when you are tired, and your spouse should show compassion and understanding. That is something the couple needs to work out a plan, such as you, the woman, taking an early nap to regenerate before going to sleep for the night or provide your knight with intimacy before getting up for your daily routine. There could also be times when you are tired, but decide to please your husband anyway, and you unexpectedly experience the Fourth of July. As a woman of God grows in marriage, trials and tribulations will come, but never forsake intimacy. Allow the Spirit of God to guide you through the process and continue to love unconditionally. God expects His daughters to exhibit His characteristics of love in all situations, especially in marriage.

Support your husband in his endeavors without the need to be competitive in the relationship. Love is kind and not envious, the Word of God states.

Charity suffereth long, and is kind; charity evieth
not; charity vaunteth not itself, is not puffed up,
doth not behave itself unseemly, seeketh not her
own, is not easily provoked, thinketh no evil;
rejoiced not in iniquity but rejoiced in the truth;
1 Corinthians 13:4-6

Let these thoughts abound within you as you relate to your spouse. First Peter 4:8-10 talks about how love covers a multitude of sins and extends the same love God extends to us. A woman of God extending this love to her husband will break down many walls and repair a broken relationship. Allow your husband to shine and provide the support needed for his success.

When the children come, work together as a team, but when disagreements arise, allow your husband to execute his role as a father and disciplinarian. If, however, your husband expresses abusive or violent behavior, address the situation immediately and seek outside help to ensure the children's safety. If your husband makes a decision and you disagree, address your concern in private and not before the children. For example, if your husband tells one of the children, "You cannot go to a friend's house," but you see no reason for the denial, do not undermine his decision. Teamwork is critical when a husband and wife are rearing their children. The most disruptive family dynamic is when a father and mother manipulate each other for the child's approval or the child manipulates the parents against each other to get their desires. A healthy family dynamic is needed for the safety and security of a family. Children need to know there are boundaries and the parents are working together to ensure family unity. A wife and mother who loves God will allow the Holy Spirit to lead and guide her to do what is right in His eyes. Sometimes, God's directions are not the desire of a Christian woman, but a God-fearing woman submits and looks back with no regrets about following God's directions.

I read an article on Family Life titled "Happily Married? A 10-Step Relationship Assessment" by Janel Breitenstein.[5] The article posed a ten-question assessment regarding marriage and relationships with a spouse:

1. "How do I respond to my spouse?"
2. "Where is your spouse (and marriage) on your priority list?"
3. "How much do I respect my spouse?"
4. "How would I describe our sex life?"
5. "How 'together' are we emotionally, spiritually, physically, and socially?"
6. "Do we practice kindness and generosity—even when we're ticked?"
7. "How committed are we to each other?"
8. "How thankful are we for each other?"
9. "Are we living for something beyond ourselves?"
10. "How willing are we to forgive each other?"

The assessment is for couples to take, but the work begins with you as a woman who both fears and loves God. Judge your role in the relationship and let peace begin with you. A woman cannot change her husband, but she can change the way she reacts to him with God's Holy Spirit.

Conflicts will arise in marriage and your reactions will determine the outcomes. A Christian woman is challenged in this area due to her willingness to obey the Holy Spirit and not her will. You may feel like you are giving the most and not receiving much in return; be led by the Holy Spirit. Love when you do not feel like loving and when the individual does not deserve it. Think on Christ's love for us, especially the undeserved love He has bestowed upon you. Do not seek revenge and remember 1 Peter 3:9, *Not rendering evil for evil, or railing for railing: but contrariwise blessing; knowing that ye are thereunto call that ye should inherit a blessing.* Pray to the Father that your husband will allow the peace of God to dwell in and keep his eyes on heavenly things.

You must also pray that God gives you a clean heart so you will have the ability to hear from heaven and surrender to the Holy Spirit. I believe Tamela Mann's song "Change Me" says it best, stating ones seeking to be more Christlike to worship God. This song was inspirational in my life and helped me to focus on my relationship with God instead of trying to change my husband. When you start to change your prospective and keep your eyes on Christ, you can have the peace of God that passes all understanding.

In due time, God will show you His mighty hands upon your life.

Chapter 3

Career

When a woman loves God, she must seek the direction from God regarding a career. If she has a special career interest, seek God's approval. Seeking God's approval will eliminate several major changes and one's contentment in their career. Many women only look at the monetary advantages in some career fields and make their decision totally on that aspect. After many years in the field of their choice, they find no contentment or satisfaction in their job. Many women leave their job and look for the career or job they feel that God is calling them to do. Others remain in their job and become angry, bitter, and resentful employees. This, in turn, carries over into their home and affects their family life.

If you identify with the last statement, seek direction from God, and do not change until you know that He is directing you to make a career change. If the change is based on a hidden agenda, craftiness, or personal gain, please reconsider how much God can truly help you find wholeness and fulfillment in your work while also serving Him. The change should be based upon doing the will of the Father in heaven and pleasing Him. Remember Proverbs 3:5-6, *Trust in the Lord with all thine heart; and lean not unto thine own understanding. In all thy ways acknowledge him, and he shall direct thy paths.*

There are many examples of Christian women in the Bible with an occupation, which we will look more into shortly. They are dedicated and obedient to God's directive. It is all about priority and what is most important to you. I went back to college to work on my master's degree when my youngest child was two years old and the others were five and seven. My husband and I would get them ready for bed at night, and once they were settled in, I would work on my academic assignments. On the weekends, my husband would keep the children occupied while I went to the public library to complete my assignments.

One semester, I had a class where assignments were due during the week. My daughter, my second and the only girl between two boys, came home with her hair full of sand one evening during this time. I tried my best to comb out the sand, but to no avail. My paper was due that night and I went into a panic mode. The Holy Spirit reminded me that my daughter was my first priority, so I took out her braids, washed, and rebraided her hair. After putting her to bed, I worked on my assignment and completed it in record time because I was obedient to the Holy Spirit and to my job as a mother.

Many women in the Bible were mentioned by name and their occupation. These women brought honor to God in their jobs and to the advancement to His kingdom. The women were respected and admired in their communities such as Shiphrah and Puah, midwives (Exodus 1:8-22),

Deborah, judge and warrior (Judges 4:4-5), Huldah, teacher (2 Kings 22:14-20), Esther, queen (Esther 4) Mary, housewife or domestic engineer (Luke 1:46-55), Lydia, businesswoman (Acts 16:14), Priscilla, tentmaker (Acts 18: 2-3), and Tabitha or Dorcas, seamstress and philanthropist (Acts 9:36). These are just to name only a few.

When a Christian woman works outside of the home, she needs to be mindful of the message she gives to the world, the fruits of the Spirit, not of the flesh (Galatians 5:16-26). I am not advocating being a doormat, but addressing concerns with Christ-like behaviors. It is difficult sometimes to exhibit these behaviors, but the Holy Spirit is there to guide His children, if we allow. If you mess up, just ask for forgiveness and apologize.

I remember working with a co-worker who always exhibited a negative attitude and would approach others in a demeaning manner. For a few years, I would state my concern in a non-confrontational matter or overlook the behavior; however, she approached me one day with a concern in a hostile manner, and I couldn't help but respond the same way. After the conversation was over, I began to work on another project, but was convicted by the Holy Spirit. I knew I needed to apologize for the way I expressed myself. Yes, I could justify my response, but it did not edify who I claimed to be in Christ. So, I went to my co-worker and apologized for the way I responded. My co-worker indicated there was no need to apologize, but I insisted. We need to be the light of the world.

Ye are the light of the world. A city that is set on a hill cannot be hid... Let your light so shine before men, that they may see your good works, and glorify your Father which is in heaven.
Matthew 5:14,16

Are we the light of the world in our career? When placed in a difficult situation and a supervisor is indirectly persuading you to think like the world, what do you do? You know the company policies and you know you may please your supervisor by agreeing and not violating policies. Do you just provide enough information to the customer and selectively leave out other options? You know the customer does not have the knowledge and support from others to know the total truth. God expects His children to exhibit characteristics that glorify Him.

As a school counselor, I saw many challenges the students had to face. Some they had no control over while others were created by decisions they had made. I know I could not teach them the Word of God, but I could allow His love to radiate in me through my actions.

Several years ago, one of my students became pregnant and I was put in a challenging situation. My supervisor wanted me to tell the student to leave the school and go to a program that was about twenty miles away, but the ride alone would take about forty-five minutes due to traffic. The program had many benefits for pregnant girls and students could remain at their zone school with marginal support. I was indirectly advised not to mention the latter option, but I was completely honest with the student. I contacted a district personnel over teen pregnancy to speak with the student and provided all resources available to the student. We would have conversations about not giving up on school and how high school would provide more options to continue her education. I knew she was having a difficult time as her body was changing with her baby's development and her mind was dealing with negative comments from her peers.

As the years passed, I often thought of the student when someone would ask me about teenage pregnancy. One day, I was at the administrative building of the school and said hello to one of my co-workers helping a parent. The parent stated that she knew me and asked my co-worker for a private minute with me. She told me she had been searching for me, but was unable to find me. She was not able to see my face that day due to my face mask (this was during the second year of the COVID-19 pandemic), but she knew my voice. She told me she was the student who had been pregnant and I was responsible for her success. At that moment, all I could do was hug her tight. She indicated things had been difficult, but she was working at a hospital and going to school to become a nurse, and her child was currently attending the school there.

Women glorify God through their words and actions. An article written by Derek Hill in What Christians Want to Know, "How To Glorify God At Work: 7 Help Tips,"[6] indicated the following tips:

1. "Work unto the Lord"–Whatever job you are given, give it your best
2. "Be Punctual" – This shows integrity
3. "Encompass the Fruits of the Spirit"–Galatians 5:22-23

4. "Be Creative"–Find ways to improve the processes at work
5. "Always Speak the Truth"–People can depend on and trust you
6. "Pray Before Lunch"–Express your love for God and be a witness to others
7. "Stand for Christ"–Remain loyal to God at all times, even if it stops a promotion

Chapter 4

Empty Nest

A Christian mother prepares her children to become independent adults. During that process, a mother teaches her children obedience, love, and the fear of the Lord (Ephesians 6:4). She also remembers Proverbs 22:6, *Train up a child in the way he should go: and when he is old, he will not depart from it*. It can sometimes be a struggle for a mother to let go of her children, but she knows it is important for their development into adulthood. She needs to pray for their protection daily and for God to provide her with other tasks to occupy her time. She can invest more time to build a closer relationship with her husband, or if not married, more time investing in the things of God. Married or unmarried, she should embrace one or two activities outside of the home she may have stopped due to becoming a mother.

If you find yourself in this chapter of your life, embrace it and focus on becoming all you can be in Christ Jesus. Take this time to pamper yourself and enjoy being a woman on a mission for God. Many opportunities were limited due to your obligation as a mother; embrace the newfound freedom with God's directions.

Start exercising regularly and eating well to enhance your physical and mental well-being. Mothers have usually spent the last twenty-something years focusing primarily on their children and their well-being, having become lost in the shuffle of motherhood. You would not exchange the experience and guidance you provided, but less is needed at this juncture. You will always be their mother, but with less intervening and swaying over their lives. A Christian mother does not want to hinder her child's progress due to her fears, loneliness, and disappointments. She needs to pick up her cross and allow God to direct her path.

> *Trust in the Lord with all thine heart; and lean not unto thine own understanding. In all thy ways acknowledge him, and he shall direct thy paths.* Proverbs 3:5-6

I was told of a mother who would not stop interfering in her adult children's lives. She would play the part of judge and jury in their relationships with their spouses. There was one situation one of her sons-in-law dropped off one of her daughters at her home to participate in a sporting activity. The son-in-law returned late to pick up her daughter and the mother told her son-in-law to go home because her daughter was sleeping. This kind of interference can cause conflict in any marriage and a negative relationship with a mother-in-law. The mother needed to find something beyond her children to occupy her time and energy. The Word of God speaks clearly on this subject and all well-meaning individuals need to take heed to Matthew 19:6. *Wherefore they are no more twain, but one flesh. What therefore God hath joined together, let not man put asunder.*

Sometimes, a mother may see her relationship with her present or prior husband in her children's relationship with their spouses. If the relationship was one that lead to separation or divorce, the hurt or disappointment a mother experienced may unconsciously or consciously transfer into her interference and cause more havoc in her children's marriages. If a mother feels she needs to say something, she needs to be fair and equitable to the couple as a whole and not only side with her child. The wisdom of Solomon in 1 Kings 3:16-28 and prayer are essential truths when it comes to approaching and counseling the couple.

An article published in Our Daily Bread, "Preparing For An Empty Nest"⁷ puts all aspects of the empty nest syndrome into the proper prospective. The article is direct and inspirational for believers to evaluate their feelings and ask God to provide peace and guidance on the next chapter of their Christian journey.

Chapter 5

Nutrition and Exercise

Before we continue, I am not a healthcare professional. I am only giving my outlook and experiences in this area. I recommend speaking with your doctor before starting any weight loss process or any drastic changes to your diet.

As women age, their metabolism changes and causes difficulties maintaining their desired weight. Women try many quick-fix diets and even surgery to obtain their desired weight. Many achieve their goal without continual success. Research data indicates a large percentage of women regain their weight back within two years according to an article written by Daniel Engber for the Scientific American.[8]

Christian women must stop using food for comfort; look to the Creator for comfort instead. Love the body God has given you regardless of what others are saying and be confident with who you are in Jesus Christ.

Casting all your care upon him, for he careth for you. 1 Peter 5:7

Cast thy burden upon the Lord, and he shall sustain thee... Psalm 55:22

Be careful for nothing, but in every thing by prayer and supplication with thanksgiving let your requests be made known unto the God. And the peace of God, which passeth all understanding, shall keep your hearts and minds through Christ Jesus. Philippians 4:6-7

My sisters in Christ, whatever you are using to find comfort, food and beyond, remember Psalm 121:1-2, *I will lift up mine eyes unto the hills, from whence cometh my help. My help cometh from the Lord, which made heaven and earth.*

Evaluate the foods you are preparing and consuming. These are major factors in losing and maintaining one's weight. After careful evaluation of this area, if you are totally honest with yourself, what is your verdict? Change, change, change. This is most certainly challenging to do, but know that all things are achievable with God according to His purpose. God's purpose is for His people to take care of their bodies, which houses the Holy Spirit. Become aware of the things or situations that may trigger overeating from present or past situations. Until women deal with these issues, they may look to food, alcohol, drug, sex, shopping, or any other means. With food, it is easy to justify because food is needed to survive, just not in excess.

Be sure to get in some exercise to accompany your food preparations. A brisk thirty-minute walk five to six times a week can help you feel and look amazing. Your body is designed to release a certain chemical know as endorphins which will relax and improve your mood. Exercising in the morning has many benefits, but get it in whenever you can during the day, even if you only have time for a five-minute walk around your home or minutes to complete a few jumping jacks and push-ups.

At the moment of this writing, I needed to lose twenty pounds. I knew my body and some of the things that triggered me to overeat sweets and junk foods. For instance, believe it or not, writing this book was a trigger. This was my first time writing a book and I had to totally trust God to direct my path. He has kept His promise, but the problem came when I wanted to have control and know each step. Then came the stress followed, inevitably, by eating junk food. I was aware of the needed path to reach and maintain my weight, but I needed to totally surrender to God and walk by faith in all areas of my life to avoid depending on earthly things for comfort.

God's peace can be found throughout the Bible, and this passage was given to me through His Holy Spirit, Philippians 4:8. We must think on the things that have internal value to experience the peace of God. There will be times when you will come under attack by "breaking news" to get you off course, but continue to focus on the following, …*whatsoever things are true, whatsoever things are honest, whatsoever things are just, whatsoever things are pure, whatsoever things are lovely, whatsoever things are of good report; if there be any virtue, and if there be any praise, think on these things* (Philippians 4:8). You may get off track briefly, but do not stay off track. Finally, a reminder. Do not forget to read the Word of God daily. *Thy word is a lamp unto my feet, and a light unto my path* (Psalm 119:105). You cannot talk about it if you are not living it.

I utilized a commercial pre-planned food program with success, but regained the weight within a year. The program was easy and convenient, but learning how to buy and prepare the serving sizes to lose and maintain weight was also important to learn for overall health. First of all, what we put into our bodies determines our overall health. Second, the foods we prepare teaches our children good or negative eating habits, now and generations to come. Finally, we want to upkeep the temple God has provided, which is our body. I am not advocating everyone should wear a size one, but seek God's guidance on a comfortable weight. Most of all, physical activity is key to losing and maintaining weight.

After utilizing pre-planned food programs a few times, food and cost were no less desirable. So, I started researching for information about calorie intake and losing weight. I came across free information through Centers for Disease Control and Prevention (CDC). I think all of us have been made more aware of the CDC due to the COVID pandemic. The CDC has a category on "Healthy Weight, Nutrition, and Physical Activity,"[9] which provides a guide to start your journey. The U.S. Department of Agriculture also provides a program called "MyPlatePlan"[10] that provides a tailored food plan based on your age, sex, height, weight, and physical activity level. Both agencies provide additional resources you may use for your family to ensure they are receiving the appropriate daily nutritional balance meals. Women are usually the main individuals who prepare meals for the family, and whatever they do, their children will imitate the same preparation for their future families.

Recently, I rediscovered another support system. An app called Lose It![11] that allows you to track daily calorie intake and much more. You may download the app on your cell phone or laptop to monitor your progress. There are many different free apps out there for Apple and Android users to count calories. Be sure to take the time to find the one that works best for you.

Why do we overeat? Let us analyze this.

When there is an issue or concern in our lives, we need to figure out the underlining cause. The cause may be present or past experiences which need to be addressed. I was a school counselor for over thirty years, and when students came to me with their conflicts and concerns, the students and I tried to find the main reason for the problems. Some were evident, but many were not. After talking and analyzing the issue, we would usually find the underlying problem and search for a resolution. In the school system, we called it "conflict resolution." I found a simple definition on the Community Tool Box training website, "Conflict resolution is a way for two or more parties to find a peaceful solution to a disagreement among them. The disagreement may be personal, financial, political, or emotional."[12]

So, applying the concept of conflict resolution to overeating or indulging in high-calorie foods may cause a deep revelation. First and foremost, one must realize there is a problem in this area of their lives and own up to it. There are some battling weight issues due to medical and medication issues. May God extend His peace to you. Yet there may be times when it is not a medical issue, but a spiritual issue. We look at women who abuse alcohol, drugs, and prescription medications, among other things, and feel vindicated, but then we are in the same predicament. The Word of God states in Psalm 55:22, *Cast thy burden upon the Lord, and he*

shall sustain thee: he shall never suffer the righteous to be moved.
The beautiful part about casting your burden onto the Lord
is that you will feel relieved of the stress and anxiety. Again,
Philippians 4:6-9 give us the directions to have, find, and
keep peace.

Here are the four steps to conflict resolution:

1. Find out what the issue is and explore it
2. What is the need or desirer?
3. Explore alternatives
4. Agree on an action plan

These steps will assist you in making a decision to deal
with the concern and not use food for comfort. After identi-
fying the problem, pray and ask God for direction on how to
deal with it, you may not like the answer. The answer may be
forgiveness of self or others, contentment of what you have
and appreciate, live a lifestyle pleasing to God, and more.
Then read Philippians 4:6. Make your request known to
God and seek His wisdom on how to deal with the problem.
Explore many ways to address the issue/s and, please, bring
them before God for directions. Finally, create a concrete
action plan to address the concern(s) and the weight of
each concern.

Many women have struggled with weight concerns
starting at different stages of their lives from childhood,
adolescence, childbearing, young adult, and middle age.
Whatever period this started in your life, look back or look
now and analyze the circumstances. Do not blame others
even if they contributed, but force on forgiveness and move
forward with Christ's help.

Chapter 6

Counseling

From the beginning of time, man has received counsel from many forms such as God, priests or spiritual leaders, respected adults, or parents. This has enabled man's survival and the ability to pass information from one generation to another. Jesus's dialogue with the woman at the well in John chapter 4 indicates the effectiveness of Christian counseling. We are not Jesus, but we follow His example by helping others to understand the truth and follow Him.

Saul in Acts 4:4-6 was on his way to Damascus to prosecute Christians and was changed due to the questions asked by the Spirit of Christ. Saul, who was later renamed Paul, became a mighty Christian warrior and spread the Gospel of Jesus Christ. In Titus 2:4-5, the Word instructs older women to counsel young women how to love their families and exhibit Christ-like behavior. Moses heeded to the counsel of his father-in-law, Jethro, who was a priest, to divide his workload (Exodus 18:14-24). Ruth listened to the counsel of her mother-in-law, Naomi, how to properly engage in a relationship with a man (Ruth 3). There are many events in the Bible where the people of God were given wise counsel from godly people. Women who are followers of Jesus Christ must receive and give wise counsel to advance to the kingdom of God.

Christian counsel is given to help direct an individual in the right direction, understand truth, and have no regrets on their Christian journey. When we allow the Holy Spirit to counsel us, we never have regrets. The Holy Spirit is that soft voice which Jesus promised before ascending back to heaven. Jesus promised the believers the Holy Spirit will live within them, guiding and comforting them. Today, the same applies if you have accepted Him as your personal Savior.

My faith in Jesus Christ was being challenged as I wrote this book and the way I understood Him to be in my life. I wanted to seek outside Christian counseling, counsel from my pastor, and counsel from my biological brother, who is a pastor; however, I felt this enormous directive from none of these support systems. The Holy Spirit continued to remind me of the directive that was given to me to love and that I knew His Word. I even ventured to the public library to the religious section to gain more understanding of my faith. As I was perusing and seeking information, I was reminded again through the Holy Spirit, "You know My Word." All I could do was stop, cry, and surrender to God's truth. I wanted an easy way out of my situation, but God was teaching me how to be obedient to His truth and to trust Him. This situation required me to walk by faith and not my sight. I am not recommending this form of counseling for everyone, but this situation, for me, required this method.

There have been times I have sought the counsel of a godly individual, and it was much needed and appreciated.

In some situations, it will be totally between God and you. The last directive I received regarding my situation was from Exodus 14:13, ...*stand still, and see the salvation of the Lord...* I shared this Word of God to a trusted believer, and they directed me to the next passage, Exodus 14:14, *The Lord shall fight for you, and ye shall hold your peace.* When you are a verbal individual about your feelings, holding your peace can be difficult, ...*to obey is better than sacrifice...* (1 Samuel 15:22). My faith has increased through this challenging situation on my Christian walk with the Lord, and I am still learning how to totally lean and depend on Him.

Early in my Christian walk, I had a mother who loved the Lord. She would counsel me about the ways of God. She would encourage me on "being better than that." What she meant by this was to not succumb to the level of ungodly behaviors due to others' actions. She would also remind me when I started to whine or complain by saying, "Must Jesus bare the cross alone and all the world go free?" We all will have crosses on this journey. She would counsel me about things of life I did not understand at that time, but looking back, I am now thankful for her godly wisdom.

Some experiences in one's life may require outside Christian counseling, consultation with your minister, or other god-fearing women. Whatever is needed, pursue it to find the peace of God that passes all understanding (Philippians 4:7). Having godly people in your life who will tell you the truth in love and who are truly concerned about your relationship with the Lord. Remember, everybody who attends church or says they are a Christian, their motive or talk may conflict with the Word of God. Pray and ask God to direct you to an individual who will help you and strengthen you in the things of God.

Lastly, find a Sunday school and Bible study class that will enhance your understanding of God's Word and His will for your life. Statistically, Sunday school classes are the least attended on Sunday mornings. Many people will attend the morning or afternoon services, but rob themselves of the interactions with fellow believers during Sunday school. You will be pleasantly surprised how a situation you are facing may be addressed without anyone's presented knowledge. This is a form of counseling, believers encouraging and helping each other in the things of God.

In my career as a school counselor, I have seen many problems students, parents, faculty, and staff faced. It was always my pleasure to assist and encourage individuals to see the truth and their value as a human being. I was limited in giving them the Word of God, but demonstrated to them His love in me by my authentic interactions with them.

A woman must understand how to forgive, and heal from past and present situations to become a beacon of light to the things of God. This light will enable you to have godly relationships and interactions with others. You may fall or deviate from the path you know is pleasing to God; forgive yourself and ask for sincere forgiveness and strength from God. Godly counsel is critical and needed as we encounter many hardships and struggles on this Christian journey.

Conclusion

*As **women live*** for God on this Christian journey, remember the virtuous woman in Proverbs 31:10-31 can enlighten one's understanding of a godly woman. It speaks of her value in and outside of the home. Ultimately, verse 30 focuses on her relationship with God and blessings that proceed. Likewise, the woman in Titus 2:3-5 focuses on the responsibility of older women as a leader and teacher of younger women not only in words, but deeds. Christian women are obligated to glorify God is every aspect of their lives.

Writing this book is evidence of walking by faith, not by sight. Hebrews 11:1, *Now faith is the substance of things hoped for, the evidence of things not seen.* My faith in God required me to trust, believe, and obey the path God had prepared for me. Sometimes during my quiet time with the Lord, walking in the mornings, middle of the night, or conversations with others evoked the other chapters or additional information for this book. Like the virtuous and Titus women, we are called to inspire others through many dimensions of life to uplift others and give hope through Jesus Christ.

My prayer is that each individual reading this book become inspired to do what God is calling you to do and not allow fear to "cripple" you (2 Timothy 1:7). We are the salt and light of this world (Matthew 5:13-14), so let us go forth and do God's will for our lives knowing that God loves and values us in His kingdom.

That if thou shalt confess with thy mouth the Lord Jesus, and shalt believe in thine heart that God hath raised him from the dead, thou shalt be saved. For with the heart man believeth unto righteousness; and with the mouth confession is made unto salvation. Romans 10:9-10

Notes

1. Hammond, Michelle, *What To Do Until Love Finds You*, 23.

2. The Praying Woman, "7 Dating Principles Single Christian Women Should Apply Daily" https://theprayingwoman.com/7-dating-principles-single-christian-women-should-apply-daily/2/.

3. Jacobs, Joy and Strubel, Deborah, Single, Whole & Holy, Christian Women and Sexuality, "Planning to Fail or Failing to Plan?", 36-38.

4. Florea, Alex, "6 Characteristics of a Healthy Singles Ministry", Boundless, Focus on the Family, https://www.boundless.org/blog/6-characteristics-of-a-healthy-singles-ministry/.

5. Breitenstein, Janel, "Happily Married? A 10-Step Relationship Assessment" Family Life, https://www.familylife.com/articles/topics/marriage/staying-married/happily-married-a-10- step-relationship-assessment/.

6. Hill, Derek, "How To Glorify God At Work: 7 Helpful Tips", What Christians Want to Know, https://www.whatchristianswanttoknow.com/how-to-glorify-god-at-work-7-helpful-tips/.

7. "Preparing For An Empty Nest". Our Daily Bread, https://ourdailybread.org/article/preparing-for-an-empty-nest/.

8. Engber, Daniel, Unexpected Clues Emerge About Why Diets Fail, https://www.scientificamerican.com/article/unexpected-clues-emerge-about-why-diets-fail/#

9. "Healthy Weight, Nutrition, and Physical Activity" Centers of Disease Control and Prevention (CDC), https://www.cdc.gov/healthyweight/losing_weight/getting_started.html.

10. "MyPlatePlan" U.S. Department of Agriculture, https://www.myplate.gov/myplate-plan.

11. Lost It, https://www.loseit.com

12. Conflict Resolution, https://ctb.ku.edu/en/table-of-contents/implement/provide-information-enhance-skills/conflict-resolution/main#:~:text=Conflict%20resolution%20is%20a%20way,negotiation%20to%20resolve%20the%20disagreement.

CPSIA information can be obtained
at www.ICGtesting.com
Printed in the USA
BVHW05050920623
666137BV00003B/70